ELLE FANNING

By Amy Davidson

Gareth Stevens
Publishing

RIGHT ON!

Please visit our website, www.garethstevens.com. For a free color catalog of all our high-quality books, call toll free 1-800-542-2595 or fax 1-877-542-2596.

Library of Congress Cataloging-in-Publication Data

Library of Congress Cataloging-in-Publication Data

Davidson, Amy, 1988-
 Elle Fanning / Amy Davidson.
     p. cm. — (Rising stars)
 Includes bibliographical references and index.
 ISBN 978-1-4339-7281-2 (pbk.)
 ISBN 978-1-4339-7282-9 (6-pack)
 ISBN 978-1-4339-7280-5 (library binding)
 1. Fanning, Elle, 1998—Juvenile literature. 2. Motion picture actors and actresses—United States—Biography—Juvenile literature. 3. Television actors and actresses—United States—Biography—Juvenile literature. 4. Models (Persons)—United States—Biography—Juvenile literature. I. Title.
 PN2287.F326D38 2013
 791.4302'8092—dc23
 [B]

                                    2012011872

First Edition

Published in 2013 by Gareth Stevens Publishing
111 East 14th Street, Suite 349
New York, NY 10003

Copyright © 2013 Gareth Stevens Publishing

Designer: Ben Gardner
Editor: Ryan Nagelhout

Photo credits: Cover and all backgrounds Shutterstock.com; cover, p. 1 Lester Cohen/ WireImage/Getty Images; pp. 5, 19, 21 Frazer Harrison/Getty Images; p. 7 Frederick M. Brown/ Getty Images; p. 9 Gregg DeGuire/Getty Images; p. 11 Joe Seer/Shutterstock.com; p. 13 SGranitz/WireImage/Getty Images; p. 15 J. Vespa/WireImage/Getty Images; p. 17 © iStockphoto.com/GYI NSEA; p. 23 Michael Loccisano/Getty Images; p. 25 John Shearer/Getty Images; p. 27 Jason Merritt/Getty Images; p. 29 Charles Eshelman/ Getty Images.

Printed in the United States of America

CPSIA compliance information: Batch #CS12GS: For further information contact Gareth Stevens, New York, New York at 1-800-542-2595.

Contents

Meet Elle

Elle Fanning is an actress and model.
She has acted in movies since she
was 2 years old!

5

Elle's full name is Mary Elle Fanning.

She was born on April 9, 1998.

She is from Conyers, Georgia.

7

Family Business

Elle has an older sister named Dakota. Dakota is a movie star. Elle has acted in movies with Dakota. Elle first acted in the movie *I Am Sam* in 2001.

Elle played a young form of Dakota's character in movies and on TV. In 2002, Elle starred with Dakota in the TV series *Taken*.

11

On Her Own

Elle first acted without her sister in 2003. She played Jamie in the movie *Daddy Day Care*.

13

Elle starred in the movies *The Nutcracker in 3D* and *Because of Winn-Dixie*. She was even the voice of a character in the animated movie *Astro Boy*.

In 2008, Elle starred as Phoebe

in the movie *Phoebe in Wonderland*.

Super Success

In 2011, Elle played Alice Dainard in a movie called *Super 8*. It made more than $260 million worldwide!

19

Elle was nominated for a Teen Choice Award for *Super 8*. She was so young when the movie was made she lost three baby teeth during filming!

Elle played Lily Miska in
We Bought a Zoo in 2011. In the
movie, she worked with actors
Matt Damon and Scarlett Johansson.

Scarlett Johansson

23

Hollywood Honors

People think Elle is a great actress.
In 2011, she won a Spotlight Award
for her work in *Super 8* and
We Bought a Zoo.

25

Television, Too

Elle has acted in TV shows like *House*. She has also appeared on *Law & Order: Special Victims Unit* and *Criminal Minds*.

Model Student

Elle is also a famous model, just like her big sister! She attends fashion shows all over the world. She loves clothes!

Timeline

1998   Elle is born on April 9.

2001   Elle first acts in *I Am Sam*.

2003   Elle acts in her first movie without her sister Dakota, *Daddy Day Care*.

2005   Elle stars in *Because of Winn-Dixie*.

2008   Elle plays Phoebe in *Phoebe in Wonderland*.

2011   Elle stars in *Super 8* and *We Bought a Zoo*.

For More Information

Books

Tieck, Sarah. *Dakota Fanning: Talented Actress*. Edna, MN: ABDO Publishing, 2010.

Websites

Elle Fanning

www.imdb.com/name/nm1102577

Find out more about Elle Fanning's movies.

Fanning World

fanningworld.com

This site has been supporting the Fanning sisters since 2006.

Totally Elle

www.elle-fanning.net

Stay up to date on Elle with her biggest fans on the web!

Glossary

animated: a kind of movie that looks like a cartoon

award: a prize given for doing something well

fashion: popular clothes worn a certain way

model: a person whose job is to show clothes or other things for sale

worldwide: all around the world

Index